PRAISE

M000317125

Not only lingual sensitivity to the mystery of mystery but her courage in *Separation Anxiety* to probe uncertainty with aplomb, Janice Lee is that rare lingual artist having the courage to defy while engaging uncertainty and the brinksmanship that teems with anonymity. These are poems that reconnoiter their own dispossession.

— WILL ALEXANDER, AUTHOR OF *THE COMBUSTION CYCLE*

Simultaneously visionary in scope and distilled to the barest truth in language, Janice Lee's *Separation Anxiety* journeys past death, opening to what always already was and to possibility. Notions of life, kinship, and love expand beyond species and the space-time continuum, transforming through encounter and relation. There's an intimacy and directness in these poems that carries the reader tenderly through each revelation. Whispers from the cosmos, from beloveds, and from deep inside. You'll want to meander in and revisit the world these poems build, seeing our own more sharply and with all its ghostings.

— MEGAN KAMINSKI, AUTHOR OF *GENTLE WOMEN*

In *Separation Anxiety*, we embark with the knowledge that ghosts contain an echo to listen for and intuition is a form of sight. Both an astute guide and a fellow wanderer in the liminal landscape of anticipatory grief, Janice Lee observes, 'sometimes one must choose death/ not to run away from life.' Living fully requires embracing transformation—of those we love and of ourselves. She admits, 'it is brutal,' but qualifies, 'it being linear time.' As we stop resisting mortality and linearity, we simultaneously transcend their illusion; 'we will all go down these paths/ more than once.' Navigating the territory of despair and denial without becoming consumed, Lee invites us to wake, forget, and wake again, to clear our vision and 'look around/ rather than/ ahead.'

— TERESA K. MILLER, NATIONAL POETRY
SERIES–WINNING AUTHOR OF *BORDERLINE FORTUNE*

Janice Lee's brilliance in fiction now enters poetry in this exploration of grief, love, and communication between species: human, dog, ghost. These poems are intimate as they are intellectual, full of wisdom as much as wonder. Lee makes meaning of living, dying, and the subtle, gorgeous surprise. I love this book. It makes language and the world feel new.

— LEE HERRICK, AUTHOR OF *SCAR AND FLOWER*

A delicate constellation of lives both human and not that keep threatening to come together to form meaning but then, with each new section, changes shape, continuing to open up. *Imagine a Death* is an illuminating exploration of radical intersubjectivity, the understanding that even though everyone and everything potentially can touch everything else, nothing accumulates with narrative neatness. Through brilliantly complex sentences, Lee offers a disjunctive synthesis on the multifold possibilities and fears of being.

— BRIAN EVENSON, AUTHOR OF *EILEE*

SEPARATION ANXIETY

JANICE LEE

CL◢SH

Copyright © 2022 by Janice Lee

Cover by Matthew Revert

ISBN: 978-1-955904-08-7

clashbooks.com

Troy, NY

for Benny & Maggie

How other kinds of beings see us matters. That other kinds of beings see us changes things.

— Eduardo Kohn

If we are interested in livability, impermanence, and emergence, we should be watching the action of landscape assemblages. Assemblages coalesce, change, and dissolve: this is the story.

— Anna Lowenhaupt Tsing

Death needs a new cosmology. Death is not a black hole where things cease to be. If you want to live well, keep death close. Hope includes hopelessness and grieving is showing gratitude for that which has been lost. What would it be like to treat grief as power? Even our hopelessness as a form of decomposing and falling away that is sacred.

— Bayo Akomolafe

SEPARATION ANXIETY

귀
ear

귀신
ghost

눈
eye

눈치
intuition/tact/awareness

I

1

it is the desire to make meaning
that thaws the ice
an accommodation to disruption
an accommodation to catastrophe
a desire for legacy
that is all-encompassing
despite unraveling

2
___

it hasn't been
the hotter summers

if you lose your cover
you can justify anything

I can justify anything

half into the future
is a kind of disappearance

a dying moosh
between the blades of grass
the kind of in-between existence
when you can't turn away
when the ancestors appear
your destiny in their hand
the moosh is dying
maybe tonight
a pained existence
or ritual / of belonging
this is an archive that will never last

4

we couldn't get into the garden
he said
she said
there was a wall
they said
the wall *walls*
said
the circumstances of the event itself
within the wound
there is always
a wall
but it didn't just appear there
overnight
an attempt
to track the source
of relief
of *walling*
the plants may have protested
but no one listens to what sounds
like silence
silence is conceived
perceived
said the false picture of edges
along the graceful trail
lightened
penetrated
said

said
said
and the trees weren't heard
and the wall persists
because
that's the way it is
he said
she said
it's always been that way
they said
the tree *trees*
said
the unsaid

5

it was the end
like a foxtail
caught in my dog's paw
you just went with it
that's right
precautions must be taken
a mutual friend seems to be an expert
in right & wrong
I just went with it
you weren't any different

6

have you noticed
all of the shocked faces of others
when you aren't able to learn the lesson
that you are teaching others?
when there's snow
you can cover/smooth the way
as in
it's colder now
as in
what you eat
is tied to the cow that graces
slowly
contemplating
the uncertainty of what comes next

only the cows have the time
to think so extensively about time
you might look less at your palm
if you could recall
the density
of the forest

7

the world is not a place

the area could transform
said
the openness of an open space

the area could be transformed
he said

and there
it was all tied to a cow
as they've always done
or at least
as they've always remembered

8

we exist in relation to—
or, we shuddered
as forever stared back
our demons think something has gone
귀신, gone
layered on thin
once we lost it all forever
even as we trained ourselves
to need the animal
less
no need
to gaze softly
even if you are going to be cutting it
all down

9

ometimes one must choose death
ot to run away from life
ut in order to live and not lose oneself
o an endurance of fraud and performance —
      the fish quietly swimming / that living archive of / *run away / don't run away*
— with his last gasps of air,
e screamed out:
t me live, let me finally live
nd as the last exhale slowly left his lips
e was, finally, able to live
he price of freedom when the knots that have been tied
on't know how to be
ntangled

10

we are speeding towards
where we step
where one world was
another dies, in its place
we are speeding towards
the kind of feelings
fossilized next to your defenses
can't
feel it
rather
it's convenient how we can tuck millions of years
into the speed of it all
in order for anything to make sense
everything needs to be in everything
and yet I outrun myself
every time

11

I spent all my time
within the walls
of time
I spent years of time
diving down
below the smooth stone
I spent all the clocks
watering them like moss
do I sleep here?
is this *normal*?

I can't tell anymore
I just can't tell

what is the reason that you can live so free of care?

12

---

your hand is still warm
where I refuse to let go
I mistake my own reluctance
for your warmth
and want to hold on even tighter
fearing that if I let go
I will unravel, like so many times you said I would

an alarm goes off
telling me it is time to feed my dead dog
his medications

when I am finally unhanded
I feel the weight of a crisp waterfall
like a carefully pressed flower left
between the pages of a book
by my mother's favorite poet

where did those words go?
and why can't I remember the sounds they make?

13

a hesitation
is not always indicative
of what you think it is
a pause
as such
is not always
a *pause*
an acknowledgment of the way
that humans see time
subjunctive & conditional
but it can also simply be
without pause
without hesitation
without notions of discontinuity
commas don't exist in nature
neither does your own discomfort
change the way
the wind blows

14

_____

why, the prayer
why, the wind between the rolling weeds
he calls it smog, his eyes don't hurt yet
wild sunflowers along the freeway still turning
towards the sun
still turning towards the flames
while we turn our backs
or have turned them already
waiting for redemption
that was never the point
why, we ask
as if we deserve answers
when we never listened hard enough
when we ran away from our own selves
expecting to find a home
not in ashes

15

_____

the sky makes space then takes it away
NO I don't know where you went
but
the notion of revelation is dangerous
it is brutal
it being linear time
I am only
frag
ment
ed
because
the
default
is *you*
and I
am not
a
default
body

still,
neither
are
you

16

dog fellow distance

horse is the same as *hyacinth* depending
on who is translating
magnificent horse
magnificent seer

in a dream:

(the dream is not a dream but a perceptual landing site)
(reality is not the opposite of a dream but a lens)
(the lens is not smudged but revisited)
(it is all water)
(water is not always clear but it is life)
(we do not drink water but locate it inside ourselves)

in a dream:

horse is the same as *hyacinth* depending
on the terrain

in a dream:

I step outside and my dog looks
for a place to poop
but I keep tugging
the leash

I keep telling him
hold on hold on hold on
dragging him further and further away
from the house

in a dream:

I step outside and my father
has built
wooden walkways over the lawn
wooden boxes around the plants
wooden caskets around the trees
all of the bushes and shrubs and weeds
I try to cry out NO
I open my mouth NO
I have lost my voice
it is raspy
I find my sister
I tell her
you have to tell him
NO
she tells me
tell him yourself
I say
I have no voice
I am crying and pleading with my raspy voice
I can not breathe

should we talk about the piece of turkey
in the shape
of a hammerhead shark?

17

after all that
we ended up with the right one
tilt back towards the sunrise
and when you sound out
the function
with your mouth
trace amounts of time
will vivify

place one fruit or vegetable
at each end
of the ruler

the witch's prophecy
is unexpectedly tactile

should we move around some more?

18

---

the amoebas are terrified
and all that energy
bound up
in all that *reverence*
I refuse to abandon
the words

there are more stars
in the Milky Way
than
there are grains
in ten thousand pounds of salt

let's be honest with ourselves
what are you *not*
being shown
when you are shown
the entirety of the universe

all that domesticated salt
pristine & beloved

waiting for
all that interstitial salt

the evening is persistent

19

the sky is a reflection of the sea
not the other way around

when my dog snores
sunlight lambent on his nose
I return here
to say yes
but my boxed-up legs
just cramp up
insistently
like the cramping is necessary
an affirmation
but really, it's just a way of looking forward
into the past
an ability to reconcile
the principle
of an emergency
if nothing for you is urgent
when do we know to hurry
when do we know to keep moving

legs stretching out in various shapes
around the bodies of dogs
always accommodating the other
snoring bodies
in the darkness

we know it's a good light
if it brings out the glimmer
in the dog's eyes
that, honestly, is all I need to see
to know to keep the light on
just a bit
longer
it's a good light
looking forward
to the inevitable apocalypse
just a collection of bad dreams
that are already too familiar
to lie
in any future

20

---

of course we are already there
of course we are already dying
of course that good light sees us
but can we see ourselves?

woof
woof
woof

always ask 3 times to make sure

where is the translucence
we work
so hard to attain
it is all already everything that exists
already here
already inside myself

outside:
even the moss is frozen

21

a single crow stomping around in the tall grass
the cows still grazing, heads down with no
thought
to look up at the blazing sky
geese still flying south, or north, depending on
the particular whim
squirrels huddled around bowls of water set
out for them by humans boiling rosemary and eucalyptus
inside their homes
the light is not always light
not the darkness, darkness
when you whisper into your cupped hands
pray for all of us
the birds, the trees, the moss, the dogs, the rocks, the sky
pray for all of us
they are already praying for you

22

a cavitation speaks
too
with the susurrations of what we call
compensation

in a prophecy:

thousands of sheep and goats and camels and oxen and sons and
daughters
thousands upon thousands
bleeding in the dead of night

in a prophecy:

my head is split open with an axe
and the deterioration of mind
that was inevitable from the get-go
finally finishes its course

in a prophecy:

the ghost of my dead mother
eavesdropping as I sob willfully / woefully
because I am so afraid to be alone
that I bully everyone close to me
into caring more about themselves
than about the world

whose cruel test of faith
is all of this?

23

to constantly be a rough draft of yourself
an endless process of revision
that is becoming
that is being
that is *is*

puddled up brown
during a meditation
I admit that
I wanted to just
tear up all of the weeds
I'm sorry, always
why
am I always
so
sorry

24

the blocking
waived
streams of vertical light
wavered
I've walked through
the fog before
despite
no evidence
says, a horse
integration matters
coax them into breathing
with you
imagine the table is the earth
supporting you
and when you can hold yourself
the seasons will follow

25

_____

back up to the rim
if you can call it that

I punched & kicked my way out
all because a boy laughed at me

one morning:
a crow lands on the lawn and struts away slowly

we try to save what we know
as we head home

one morning:
a crow lands on the lawn and struts away slowly

the repetition doesn't guarantee identity
but I collect the mentions:
yes, pay attention
yes, thank you
yes, I see you
do you see me?

one morning:
a crow lands on the lawn and struts away slowly

tied to a cow

the dogs poop in unison
facing
in opposite directions
momentary alignment

and then a stone, which jumps
of its own volition
as if thrown
as if dropped
but there is no one
just the echo of its sound
as it thuds against the concrete sidewalk

eventually
it all unravels

the terrible heat
the terrible noise
is it over yet?

still
I am rising

seeding = a permutation point

I am already the healed state I am looking for

26

hearing the geese
flying overhead
what I admire most
is how much
they don't give a fuck

to *human* better
hold onto that rope
and pull

but the settlers
but the felled trees
but the lingering
but the frontier
but the ignored assertion
of killing set forth
in the ancient question
are they able to — ?

human or animal
which is more ancient?
the mutation of one
affects the other
and so, *animal*
is the newer distinction
our own friendship
is haunted
the animal is a word
time elapsed

appellation
to have already died
to have already admitted
to being ashamed
of being ashamed
foreshadowing mourning

hearing oneself being named
is a little bit
like
the apocalypse
itself

28

an animal looks at me
how to respond?
yes or no

an animal looks at me
how to respond?
yes or no

an animal responds
yes or no

29

there in the bright spot against the afternoon window
when you wake up from a nap
all squinty-eyed and part of you is still
left in the other place
there in the curtains
is also your soul
there in the sunlight streaming in
spotlighting the dust motes
there, is also your soul
in the dreams left behind
of ravaged faces, hauntings of the dead
there, in that fall into fall
leaves changing color and summer flowers
beginning to deteriorate
there, also, is your soul

30

you're stalking yourself:
why do the clouds matter?

is the sound of death
the same as the sound of dying?
to prefer *not to say* is different
than silence
in the veering
the veering
or the order that comes out of chaos
the language
that articulates what isn't said
lasting progress comes through joy
sometimes joy comes easily
sometimes joy is a choice
the other person is you

unmap and vivify

so we can see them
how we are bound by causality

the aim is to shapeshift
rather than to become complacent
in the loop

right
you're smart
but you're not awake

the pool
in my journey
was small
I couldn't track the will
because it was bound up
in so much shadow

no response

no response

no response
is still

a response
is still
information

32

doubled,
as the body
becomes stiff as granite

fair skies:
my apologies for keeping you waiting

33

a faltering step
doesn't put one behind
but back in the light

34

there are bands of energy
that dwindle & build up
reaching, horizontal

the trickster coyote ascends as a starting point
but would a doorbell be a better idea
than the knocker
in the shape of a dog's head
horizontal, reaching

how is one reminded to laugh
when the winter seems endless
when despair seems endless
when it all
seems endless
and ending it all seems easier than
reaching, up, horizontal
easier than
laughing
easier than joy

here, in winter
is the strange gift of white space

here, in winter
the coyote warns of self-sabotage

there
in between those horizontal bands
of energy
there is a lone boat
attempting to navigate through the fog
and all the while being watched
and all the while
the coyote can't believe it

let's take another look

but if we reach
horizontally
dwindling light and lolling
in the shadow
of a large mossy rock
one feels the bone structure
of the landscape
one is able to dream
and the dreams, like the rock
can be shared

what are rights when you are the dreamer?
what are dreams when you are lost
in the horizontal shadow of your own attempt to journey forward?
what is an attempt when we lurch forward?
a strange consecutive sequence that enacts
dreaming & action & cleansing,
that is
while we roam the land in that dreamspace
of fog & sense & words
might we be prompted to put intention
behind the lurching
that we will all go back down these paths
more than once
and we try to explain ourselves
but there is a scurry in the step
these steps are necessary
the sky
as horizontal as it is wide
is necessary

there is the matter of water:

the sky is a reflection of the ocean, not the other way around

and when the frog calls
he calls to others
guarding, horizontal
replenishing, horizontal
bands of energy that dissipate and rebuild
a new pond
another mossy rock
another derivation of *energy*
and when in assembly
it is the dream that is forgotten
endless effects of mouths that open and close

I must have felt as a long line of mucking in the pond
I must have felt as disembodied at the water's edge
I must have felt your despair
your reaching
and when my body volunteers
it becomes darker than this
it becomes lighter
it becomes translucent
it becomes

35

find yourself laying down
the beautiful melancholy of language is tempting
but you know already to turn away
once in awhile
and take a step in the opposite direction
you know already to laugh
after the tears
but how?

with the redaction of knowing
with all you will ever be
a steady stone
that enacts the performance of
becoming
becoming
becoming
and when Benny shifts on the floor
breathes deeply
that too
is the gesture of an entire life
endearing
its ghosts
still reaching
still: the darkness of light

God
when will we learn/unlearn it all?

36

in a particular grove of trees:
horses, horses, horses
but they are not enough:
ways of being, being, being

I need to see borders
everywhere
contamination
only exists if we
try
to contain something
that can't/won't be contained
which
is everything

foraging can be one
way of being
a deluge
an act of faith
demons gather
and want to be contained
we, too, are part of the atmosphere

just how determined
is history
to deteriorate the collaborative survival
and exponentially replicate the precocity
of self:
self as private property
self as containment
self as contaminant
self as toxic chemical
self as global catastrophe
self as fire

what about the borders
between us?
what about them?

which of the following is touch?

) . . . (

) . (

) (

)(

38

---

beauty disappears
when you decide it so

then, simply blink again

39

take away what you are able
that feeling in the bowels
caused only by the irritation of
agriculture
my tummy is upset
she said
my heart is upset
she said
I am upset
she said
the seed of a bald cypress tree
in my left pocket
throws everything off balance,
or,
it tells me that it was all off before
and teaches me how to restore it,
even if just for a moment

40

the tomato plants
teach me how to deal
with each kind of person

the puffed-up pigeon repeatedly chases off his foes
not for extra crumbs but to prove that he *can*

the pigeons
show us potential hierarchies
in the making
shifting only when we put our phones down
to encounter the pigeon
on the same ground

trust me

getting down on your knees
would do you some good
hold the intention in your belly
then,
look around
rather than
ahead

41

the light
of attention

the purpose
of coming together

42

clip out an example
quivering breathing
make some incision
some arbitrary cut
after you recall that this story begins with one
there goes another one

here is the present
this scission
this zest

unclench the teeth
quivering breathing
a false entrance
awake
we can cover only what was said today

43

sometimes a silver spoon in a mug
looks like a candle
& sometime the words become like
spaces that I've forgotten how to
navi-gate
though in a dream, I've been in these crevices before
weedy
forlorn
light
indistinguishable
foster
yellow

44

are you aware of your own regressions
of when you are not fully present
how to say *tomorrow*
in the language
of *yesterday*

45

the bearing to conspire
there are many sides
to every argument
night and day
do not always make
a legitimate composition
so the trees that exist
side by side
exist
as bodies exist

the question asked
isn't the question answered
is it night or day?
indeed
all transformation is the certainty of death

when we think of synonyms
like
death & decay
illness & disease
perhaps the two
most closely linked are
living & dying

this is redundant
a rationalization of

sunset & sunrise
a specialization of
regret & existence

I used to do many things
the underlying metaphor
is one of interest & relevance & empathy
and, over time
the difference between
rotting & decay
the difference
between trees
between bodies
between teeth
between living beings
between existence & purpose

the answer is *no*
we think our answer is *yes*

the principle resides on sacrifice
on historical circumstances
that exist
only in the microscopic
relations
among cells
the domain of the forest
again
death falls from the sky
this is progress
today I am a coward
tomorrow I am god
today I may get what I want
tomorrow, the constancy of size
and the movement
towards an end

finality

so, too: the pursuit
so, too: the impossible boundaries of death
this is a description
this is a requirement for exclusivity

incorporation
tears are useless when rigor
when reason
when attempt
when structure
when together

human hands as symbols
the specificity of destruction
to spill commitment
to diverge
to recuperate
to start over
to move on
to remain stagnant among difference
injunctions on the beauty of nature

again: finality
again: more
again: living

can't you see how the act of prayer
changes the texture of the entire room?

46

her future has washed away
consequently, many plans
to prevent flooding
are now under way
the story of containment
is a story of
self & destruction & loss
now, imagine you're at a party —

47

I am not here standing up for suffering
I am here
because I am here
when attached—
the ethical order—
it will be remembered as—
it is inconceivable—

in all of this
a nostalgia for yesterday

we have been rooting for the monster
all along
a pivotal position
in the history of apologia

48

this crisis of the mother
this crisis of the parent
this crisis of the child
this crisis of breathing heavily
this crisis of witnessing
this crisis of ownership
this crisis of meaning
this crisis of the prediction of rain
this crisis of elliptical submergence
this crisis of failing
this crisis of insistence
this crisis of the shudder, shudder, again, the shudder

no

the head
catches
is blue
had to

really though,
do you want to be free?

49

today
I wonder about the labor
of worms

50

scattertold
in the beginning there
withheld as breath, given
substantiated, if forthcoming
her eyes grow dim
in the corner of the room
with the most sun
angled derpiness due to
mouth shape, beard,
red pajamas, flappy ears
my appetite for language
has become
amorphous
sun spots as breath, withheld
its beginnings grow dim
in the corner of the eye
scattershot
in the end, here

hold up, the record's on
& the dog's already snoring
with both eyes open
a dying dog is in my arms
& all I can think about is
her shivering body
the sky
the bald eagle that circled so low
while the sand blew into my can of wine
can you sense the pending death
like I can
are you ready
the way I've been readying myself
it's just death and death and
another death
floorboards creaking
'til my teeth chatter
from intoxication or cold or
the black spots
in my vision remind me
that the ancestors
have already slit my wrists open
& healed them with light
lightness of being
little moosh,
are you ready like
I've been readying myself

all my life
wet paw prints on the floor
footsteps on the wall
one foot forward
one foot

52

the future is in the touch,
I often dream

there is no difference
between the sky, so garish
here at the end of summer
and the perfected gesture of limping
like an old dog

the first day
is related to
the last day
only in that
they are the same

as I approach the river of my sacred land
where I go for guidance
to set intention
the guide that appears at my side is Benny
until now, he has never joined me
in my journeys
the water of the river
slowly sinks into the sand
and Benny starts to dig
it's obvious, isn't it
he seems to say
what I hear is
that he will be here
even when he is no longer
here
the medicine of letting go

54

when I reach the entrance
of my middle world
there is a fire burning
I sit beside it
and wait for my healed state to appear
many approach
and with each arrival
I think, yes
you are the one
bear, crow, elephant, snail, badger, whale
even Worf appears
and I wave him away
saying
you don't belong here
as I stare into the fire
I try to breathe
and practice patience
and presence
and then the glint of a hawk's eye
and the hawk's gaze
and my mother's ghost inside the hawk inside myself
I report back
the hawk
but what my teacher asks is
who is the fire?

55

ran, ran, ran
down the hill
colors running into
sudden hearing loss
it
just
gets
better
I will
I will
I will
but you have to know something first
(nodding heart)
(nodding pigeon head)
(nodding roots)
the edge of
coming out of hibernation
offers
the perfect solution
will doesn't give you the whole scene
will wills what won't be willed
shaping it all to have the same edges
I pull out my white hairs
please curb your dogs
one by one
the containment of domestication

my hand hangs
a few inches
above the dog shit

56

the fire
then the counter-fire

at that instant
a merging of words
an abrupt return
to exist in the world
of that taste that lingers
in your mouth
(salt!)

the silence
is the face you make after you speak
is the fact that if you want birds to drop dead from the trees
the birds shall drop dead from the trees

incantation
your only star is dead
darkened

that's not the way I imagined the arrival
even so,
when will I see you again?

fish can't wait
hate it / *hate it*
up to it, that well
water, up to high tide
& I melted into the crack in the wall
& came out the other other side

the white lilac blooms at dawn

fidget

white balls of light in
my peripheral vision
dusking music
felt down to my toes
forgive me
for everything I can't remember

58

please, a little longer like this
mutely, though it has passed already
I am dying, still

59

of the rock with holes
in the center of my earth painting?

I crossed the threshold once
and then, I couldn't breathe

unmap and vivify

contact: a touch against time

of the surface, of the darkened-dark below
beneath my feet?

person moving
(there's no escape)
of distance
people
say, of distance

will you wait in line for me?

of separation anxiety
anxiety exists because separation exists
(or doesn't)
my hand is reaching for your back

the arrogance of problem-solving

what we all fear
at the core
is the loss of love & merging

where does all your shit go?

the disadvantaged cow
is happy to see you

60

the ocean water is beckoning you to jump
not as an invitation to death
but as an invitation for life
the drumbeat coming from the mountains
is already that of your heart
the ants seem happy to see me
until I press down on them with my thumb

61

as snake:
small, in the grass
exposed, vulnerable
of tinsel, of down, of softer than this
trying to reach
even the bugs look big
of wanting to burrow underground
of finding the entrance to the underworld
safety in the dark, below
everything
is waiting to happen

as jaguar:
resting, on a large rock
of watching, of being watched
presence of the heartspace
and knowing that it's not always
about being seen by another
I'm only still becoming
glint-shard of arrival
believe me, I see you

as condor:
woven of eye-glints
the watching
recognition / negotiation
fracturing / coincidence

threat / antidote
of threatening with a gaze
of stepping into the sky
and recognizing
the distance now
who feels threatened by me?

62

it's like I didn't hurt you
when you regress
I regress

my love
a lapse like lightened water
lightlessness
in dimness
in an elongated space

because she loves him

the world sleeps awaiting confirmation

63

down the river
dead on the river
stagger(s)
what I took was to show you that I could
I took it
looked up at you
I took it
with my mouth
I only remembered
when I turned on the news
but that isn't true
river winding
bending, over
the news isn't ever off
staggering
downriver

64

howl harder
that sinking gut feeling
that sinking below the soil feeling
your intestines disintegrating in the molten
heat of the earth's core
your moans of pain that can
't be heard by
anyone but the crows because you've been
stretched so thin
I remember when my mother told me to be-
-ware
all men are dogs
and to this day the one I loved the most
is an actual dog
still running along the beach waiting for the
pieces of oxtail that I chew off and save for him
when the worms get up to my knees
I feel them wriggling in that in-between space
where the soul resides
under the skin, under the kneecap
soft/chewy tendons
sometimes we need more space to get away
from that kind of love
to settle in again
back in the soil
it isn't so dark under it all
it isn't so damp, it isn't so unfamiliar

the grave we avoid everyday
is also the site of our redemption
dying is living & living is dying & both
are sacred and the worms crawling up my nose
while my corpse rots are sacred
and your bloodied knuckles still beating
against the wall are sacred
and each & every breath is sacred
it never ends
there is no finality to history, no final movement
just the eternal movement of the sun
and your knees scraping across the concrete
as you crawl tirelessly towards the horizon

65

I don't know how to be any more lovable
hinged, the freedom that is inside any single moment
ichi-go ichi-e

the geese honking as they fly overhead:
a once-in-a-lifetime encounter
the gaze of the misleading chickens:
a once-in-a-lifetime encounter
the moon is incomplete:
a once-in-a-lifetime encounter

freedom is inside there
ichi-go ichi-e
we are hinged
we are bound by causality
(today is still occupied by the past)
the endlessness claps for itself
and depth encrusts joy
and joy encrusts holding
yes
says
the holding pattern
yes
says
the river
it comes up to our knees
and I dip one hand

into the cool water
fingers graze a smooth stone
you can hold that
says the water
thank you
I say

66

commemoration can be a catastrophe
that is, climate change
is the flattening
of circular time
survival
is the question of
how to go about inhabiting a future
that has happened already
so often
I become someone I hate being
I find your presence
triggering
we are connected
intimately
but all I can think of is
dying
when I'm with you
parabiosis
is a wretched structure
there, there
it will be okay

67

I knew you were trouble
when you walked in
turn it around
I knew I was trouble
when you walked in

68

the story I'm telling myself
is that you abandoned me
but the thing is
I abandoned you
when I abandoned myself
the elements are never separated

I'm not here as a witness
every morning
I insist on imaging inadequacy *march*
why does everything have to be a death match?
the display of affection
overtakes the intention of affection
and the distance of now becomes hysterical
I pretend I can't reach you
but you are right
there

69

to trace this phantasmic body
pivot, and sustains
it shall be so
to hear what one sees
the deployment of sonorous material
articulations of honor
of *should*
planeterizing
phenomenon
of a distance
it as as if
instances
instants
holding
calm, in what time?
seeing, than in hearing
the action forever to come
after the extraction
bring in light
and harmonize

70

oh, bravery was irrelevant there
if we get separated
we'll meet back at, you know, that place

71

I throw my body against the door
but no one answers, no one is there
I throw my body into the ocean
to feel the weight of sinking
like a rock
is this the most solid I will ever be?
I tear myself apart and send all the pieces
flying into the wind
maybe one will land somewhere habitable
and sprout, while the others
find themselves stuck in a liminal corridor
where there is no time, no space, nor gravity
I remember thinking that I needed to
blow all of the seeds on the dandelion in one go,
like candles on a birthday cake,
and looking down with despair at the seeds still
clinging to the stem
all of this, I interpreted as my own failure,
my own undeservedness to exist
I throw my body into the readied grave

still, I am shaking against the dust

72

it is impossibly hard to outlive your own children

73

of tree time
of ancestral modesty
of howling in the daytime
of the unclear border of a beach
of radial kinship
of sacred discomfort
of ecology as language
of so-small, so-small
of yours and yours and mine
of pivoting and doubt
of advice and salutations and what was said
of hallucinating said-ness
as air is breathed
there is no cure
for any of it

74

nothing is dying
yes, yes, yes nods the dog
this is directly related to your understanding of the world
listen, when you lash out
I can't help but scream
arise woven like loud pistils and
I said once
that I just need you to listen
but your listening voice
keeps conjuring
all of my ghosts
I buried that shit
in the garden
used it for compost
it's just the fear
that keeps calling them back
telepathy resists barriers
but when I let the weeds grow
I forget to let my guard back down

s becoming more and more precarious
e an individual
arry the fear of losing one's dog
hout succumbing completely
levastation

at I'm working towards
his:
[image of human body with arms open & outstretched, receiving light]

er than this:
[image of human body hunched over, clenched & tight, fists closed, white knuckles]

etting the world work
ccepting the cycles of the universe
nny, I don't know how to let you go)
knowing we have already lived many lives together
ma, go now?)
he universe will know
see us together again
tempting the life sustaining posture)
not crumble & break completely
ma, it's ok)
ccept that it's not all over

just because you are leaving
I must continue loving
when you are gone

what are you actually running from
when you think you're running towards
the earth is round, so you'll end up
where you started, eventually
but will you know how to face
your history
or will you run again, another destination
disguised as a goal
how much of what you strive towards
what you call *dream*
is a manifestation of your fears
a reluctance to settle into your wounds
to do the work of seeing that entanglement
what else can you imagine for yourself
& dream into being
if you could remember to sink down
into your breath (especially if things are going to shit, *especially then*)
deterioration is transformation
& dying is still living

Which one are you:

an owl, a snake, or an orange?

a lion, a dandelion, or a salmon?

a goose, a horse, or a hyacinth?

a dog, a daisy, a donut?

a pine cone, a sock, a blade of grass?

a wave, a particle field, the prairie?

a stick in the shape of a person, a sea anemone, a stinging nettle

a fig tree, a bird bath, an acorn?

a dragonfly, a cloud, or a tomato plant?

whalesong, lightning, gravity?

an eagle, a gopher, or an earthworm?

a wheelbarrow, a bee, or a stone?

a badger, a toad, a volcano?

a mushroom, a secret, a window?

a yak, a yogurt, a daffodil?

an invitation to empathetic seeing
might begin
with the tree
might begin
with the phrase
I suppose
and the density of a forest
might begin at the edges:
blurred, unfocused

one tree falls down
and we all hear it falling
the other trees around it
rattle & shake
are affected by the other tree
are *affected*

when there is so much green
we might penetrate the picture space
and find ourselves
lost in the shades of green

when the person in front of us is dressed in blue
we might speak for them
in a bout of empathy
and find ourselves lost in the shades of blue
this is the density of color

when one has nowhere
left to go
when their back is to us
we might think
just get a grip man
and then they do
get a grip

still lost in the green
one might think
it all ends where it begins
and yet nothing begins again
the landscape is green and rain
and the body is obscured by the veil of moisture
and the green is obscured
by eyes looking
and the edges blur again as a cow moves slowly
the periphery is unreliable
the cow is unreliable
the spectator is unreliable
the rain is unreliable
empathy is unreliable

I remember the feeling of being alive
I feel something
yet find myself located here
it isn't so green here
neither am I welcomed by the intimacy of the rain
neither has it ended yet
neither has it begun

ACKNOWLEDGMENTS

Thank you to many thinkers and writers, whose writings and ideas continue to influence my relationship to the world and to language: including Etel Adnan, Bayo Akomolafe, Marisol de la Cadena, Alexis Pauline Gumbs, Eduardo Kohn, Anna Lowenhaupt Tsing, Anne Waldman.

Thank you to my friends, the brilliant influences and constellations of light in my life: Harold Abramowitz, Amanda Ackerman, Will Alexander, Teresa Carmody, Jessie Carver, Gabrielle Civil, Jenny Donovan, Sueyeun Juliette Lee, Gabriela Torres Olivares, Andrea Quaid, Michael Seidlinger, Lidia Yuknavitch, Leni Zumas.

Thank you especially to my friend, companion and collaborator Brenda Iijima.

Thank you to all of my teachers, especially Anna Joy Springer, Jon Wagner, Rosemary Beam, and Thich Nhat Hanh (Thay). Thank you also to all of my sisters at Rising Fire.

Thank you to my love Josh.

Forever gratitude to the mooshes, Benny, Maggie, Piper and all of the mooshes everywhere.

Thank you also to The Sou'wester Artist Residency Program.

Endless admiration and thanks to shining stars Leza Cantoral and Christoph Paul for everything they do.

The poem on page 85 is a reference to the lyrics of Taylor Swift's "I Knew You Were Trouble."

Earlier versions/excerpts have previously appeared in: *Anthropocene, Berfrois, Cultural Weekly, Entropy, The Gravity of the Thing, Maudlin House, Orion Magazine, Pleiades, Yes Poetry,* and *Urgent Possibilities: Writings on Feminist Poetics & Emergent Pedagogies* (eohippus labs).

ABOUT THE AUTHOR

Janice Lee (she/they) is a Korean American writer, teacher, spiritual scholar, and shamanic healer. She is the author of 7 books of fiction, creative nonfiction & poetry, most recently: *Imagine a Death* (Texas Review Press, 2021) and *Separation Anxiety* (CLASH Books, 2022). She writes about interspecies communication, plants & personhood, the filmic long take, the apocalypse, inherited trauma, and the Korean concept of han, and asks the question, how do we hold space open while maintaining intimacy? Incorporating shamanic and energetic healing, she teaches workshops on inherited trauma, healing and writing, and practices in several lineages, including the medicine tradition of the Q'ero, Zen Buddhism (in the tradition of Plum Village & Thich Nhat Hanh), and Korean shamanic ritual (Muism). She currently lives in Portland, OR where she is an Assistant Professor of Creative Writing at Portland State University.

ALSO BY JANICE LEE

Imagine a Death, Houston, TX: Texas Review Press, September 2021.

The Sky Isn't Blue: The Poetics of Spaces, Brooklyn, NY: Civil Coping Mechanisms, March 2016.

Reconsolidation: Or it's the ghosts who will answer you, Los Angeles, CA: Penny-Ante Editions, September 2015.

Damnation, Los Angeles, CA: Penny-Ante Editions, October 2013.

Daughter, Seattle, WA: Jaded Ibis Press, May 2011.

KEROTAKIS, UK: Dog Horn Publishing, May 2010.

ALSO BY CLASH BOOKS

WE PUT THE LIT IN LITERARY

CLASHBOOKS.COM

FOLLOW US

TWITTER

IG

FB

@clashbooks

CPSIA information can be obtained
at www.ICGtesting.com
Printed in the USA
JSHW031127260522
26405JS00004B/6